Book 1
C Programming Professional
Made Easy

BY SAM KEY

&

Book 2
Android Programming In a Day!

BY SAM KEY

Book 1
C Programming Professional Made Easy

BY SAM KEY

Expert C Programming Language Success In A Day For Any Computer User!

Programming Box Set #22: C Programming Professional Made Easy & Android Programming in a Day

Table Of Contents

Introduction.. 5

Chapter 1 The Basic Elements Of C 6

Chapter 2 What is C Programming Language..................................... 17

Chapter 3 Understanding C Program... 19

Chapter 4 Learn C Programming.. 21

Conclusion 32

Introduction

I want to thank you and congratulate you for purchasing the book, "Professional C Programming Made Easy: Expert C Programming Language Success In A Day For Any Computer User!".

This book contains proven steps and strategies on how to understand and perform C programming. C is one of the most basic programming tools used for a wide array of applications. Most people stay away from it because the language seem complicated, with all those characters, letters, sequences and special symbols.

This book will break down every element and explain in detail each language used in the C program. By the time you are done with this book, C programming language will be easy to understand and easy to execute.

Read on and learn.

Thanks again for purchasing this book. I hope you enjoy it!

Chapter 1 The Basic Elements Of C

The seemingly complicated C program is composed of the following basic elements:

Character Set

The alphabet in both upper and lower cases is used in C. The 0-9 digits are also used, including white spaces and some special characters. These are used in different combinations to form elements of a basic C program such as expressions, constants, variables, etc.

Special characters include the following:

+ ,. *– / % = & ! #?"^ '| / ()< > { }[ ];: @ ~!

White spaces include:

- Blank space

- Carriage return

- Horizontal tab

- Form feed

- New line

Identifiers

An identifier is a name given to the various elements of the C program, such as arrays, variables and functions. These contain digits and letters in various arrangements. However, identifiers should always start with a letter. The letters may be in upper case, lower case or both. However, these are not interchangeable. C programming is case sensitive, as each letter in different cases is regarded as separate from each other. Underscores are also permitted because it is considered by the program as a kind of letter.

Examples of valid identifiers include the following:

ab123

A

stud_name

average

velocity

TOTAL

Identifiers need to start with a letter and should not contain illegal characters. Examples of invalid identifiers include the following:

2nd - should always start with a letter

"Jamshedpur" - contains the illegal character (")

stud name - contains a blank space, which is an illegal character

stud-name - contains an illegal character (-)

In C, a single identifier may be used to refer to a number of different entities within the same C program. For instance, an array and a variable can share one identifier. For example:

The variable is int difference, average, A[5]; // sum, average

The identifier is A[5].

In the same program, an array can be named A, too.

__func__

The __func__ is a predefined identifier that provides functions names and makes these accessible and ready for use anytime in the function. The complier would automatically declare the __func__ immediately after placing the opening brace when declaring the function definitions. The compiler declares the predefined identifier this way:

static const char __func__[] = "Alex";

"Alex" refers to a specific name of this particular function.

Take a look at this example:

```c
#include <stdio.h>


void anna1(void)  {

     printf("%sn",__func__);

     return;

}


int main() {

    myfunc();

}
```

What will appear as an output will be anna1

Keywords

Reserved words in C that come with standard and predefined meanings are called keywords. The uses for these words are restricted to their predefined intended purpose. Keywords cannot be utilized as programmer-defined identifiers. In C, there are 32 keywords being used, which include the following:

auto	default
break	double
char	float
case	else
continue	extern
const	enum
do	goto

for	switch
if	typedef
long	struct
int	union
register	switch
short	void
return	unsigned
sizeof	while
signed	volatile

Data Types

There are different types of data values that are passed in C. Each of the types of data has different representations within the memory bank of the computer. These also have varying memory requirements. Data type modifiers/qualifiers are often used to augment the different types of data.

Supported data types in C include int, char, float, double, void, _Bool, _Complex, arrays, and constants.

int

Integer quantities are stored in this type of data. The data type *int* can store a collection of different values, starting from INT_MAX to INT_MIN. An in-header file, <limits h>, defines the range.

These int data types use type modifiers such as unsigned, signed, long, long long and short.

Short int means that they occupy memory space of only 2 bytes.

A long int uses 4 bytes of memory space.

Short unsigned int is a data type that uses 2 bytes of memory space and store positive values only, ranging from 0 to 65535.

Unsigned int requires memory space similar to that of short unsigned int. For regular and ordinary int, the bit at the leftmost portion is used for the integer's sign.

Long unsigned int uses 4 bytes of space. It stores all positive integers ranging from 0 to 4294967295.

An int data is automatically considered as signed.

Long long int data type uses 64 bits memory. This type may either be unsigned or signed. Signed long long data type can store values ranging from −9,223,372,036,854,775,808 to 9,223,372,036,854,775,807. Unsigned long long data type stores value range of 0 to 18,446,744,073,709,551,615.

char

Single characters such as those found in C program's character set are stored by this type of data. The char data type uses 1 byte in the computer's memory. Any value from C program's character set can be stored as char. Modifiers that can be used are either unsigned or signed.

A char would always use 1 byte in the computer's memory space, whether it is signed or unsigned. The difference is on the value range. Values that can be stored as unsigned char range from 0 to 255. Signed char stores values ranging from −128 to +127. By default, a char data type is considered unsigned.

For each of the char types, there is a corresponding integer interpretation. This makes each char a special short integer.

float

A float is a data type used in storing real numbers that have single precision. That is, precision denoted as having 6 more digits after a decimal point. Float data type uses 4 bytes memory space.

The modifier for this data type is long, which uses the same memory space as that of double data type.

double

The double data type is used for storing real numbers that have double precision. Memory space used is 8 bytes. Double data type uses long as a type modifier. This uses up memory storage space of 10 bytes.

void

Void data type is used for specifying empty sets, which do not contain any value. Hence, void data type also occupies no space (0 bytes) in the memory storage.

_Bool

This is a Boolean type of data. It is an unsigned type of integer. It stores only 2 values, which is 0 and 1. When using _Bool, include **<stdboolh>**.

_Complex

This is used for storing complex numbers. In C, three types of _Complex are used. There is the float _Complex, double _Complex, and long double _Complex. These are found in <complex h> file.

Arrays

This identifier is used in referring to the collection of data that share the same name and of the same type of data. For example, all integers or all characters that have the same name. Each of the data is represented by its own array element. The subscripts differentiate the arrays from each other.

Constants

Constants are identifiers used in C. The values of identifiers do not change anywhere within the program. Constants are declared this way:

const datatype varname = value

const is the keyword that denotes or declares the variable as the fixed value entity, i.e., the constant.

In C, there are 4 basic constants used. These include the integer constant, floating-point, character and string constants. Floating-point and integer types of constant do not contain any blank spaces or commas. Minus signs can be used, which denotes negative quantities.

Integer Constants

11

Integer constants are integer valued numbers consisting of sequence of digits. These can be written using 3 different number systems, namely, decimal, octal and hexadecimal.

Decimal system (base 10)

An integer constant written in the decimal system contains combinations of numbers ranging from 0 to 9. Decimal constants should start with any number other except 0. For example, a decimal constant is written in C as:

const int size =76

Octal (base 8)

Octal constants are any number combinations from 0 to 7. To identify octal constants, the first number should be 0. For example:

const int a= 043; const int b=0;

An octal constant is denoted in the binary form. Take the octal 0347. Each digit is represented as:

$0347 = 011\ 100\ 111 = 3 * 8^2 + 4 * 8^1 + 7 * 8^0 = 231$
--- --- ---
3   4   7

Hexadecimal constant (base 16)

This type consists of any of the possible combinations of digits ranging from 0 to 9. This type also includes letters a to f, written in either lowercase or uppercase. To identify hexadecimal constants, these should start with 0X or 0X. For example:

const int c= 0x7FF;

For example, the hexadecimal number 0x2A5 is internally represented in bit patterns within C as:

$0x2A5 = 0010\ 1010\ 0101 = 2 * 16^2 + 10 * 16^1 + 5 * 16^0 = 677$
---- ---- ----
2   A   5

Wherein, 677 is the decimal equivalent of the hexadecimal number 0x2.

Prefixes for integer constants can either be long or unsigned. A long integer constant (long int) ends with a l of L, such as 67354L or 67354l. The last portion of an unsigned long integer constant should either be ul or UL, such as 672893UL or 672893ul. For an unsigned long long integer constant, UL or ul should be at the last portion. An unsigned constant should end with U or u, such as 673400095u or 673400095U. Normal integer constants are written without any suffix, such as a simple 67458.

Floating Point Constant

This type of constant has a base 10 or base 16 and contains an exponent, a decimal point or both. For a floating point constant with a base 10 and a decimal point, the base is replaced by an E or e. For example, the constant $1.8 * 10^{-3}$ is written as 1.8e-3 or 1.8E-3.

For hexadecimal character constants and the exponent is in the binary form, the exponent is replaced by P or p. Take a look at this example:

This type of constant is often precision quantities. These occupy around 8 bytes of memory. Different add-ons are allowed in some C program versions, such as F for a single precision floating constant or L for a long floating point type of constant.

Character Constant

A sequence of characters, whether single or multiple ones, enclosed by apostrophes or single quotation marks is called a character constant. The character set in the computer determines the integer value equivalent to each character constant. Escape sequences may also be found within the sequence of a character constant.

Single character constants enclosed by apostrophes is internally considered as integers. For example, 'A' is a single character constant that has an integer value of 65. The corresponding integer value is also called the ASCII value. Because of the corresponding numerical value, single character constants can be used in calculations just like how integers are used. Also, these constants can also be used when comparing other types of character constants.

Prefixes used in character constants such as L, U or u are used for character literals. These are considered as wide types of character constants. Character literals with the prefix L are considered under the type wchar_t, which are defined as <stddef.h> under the header file. Character constants that use the prefix U or u are considered as type char16_t or char32_t. These are considered as unsigned types of characters and are defined under the header file as <uchar.h>.

Those that do not have the prefix L are considered a narrow or ordinary character constant. Those that have escape sequences or are composed of at least 2 characters are considered as multicharacter constants.

Escape sequences are a type of character constant used in expressing non-printing characters like carriage return or tab. This sequence always begins with a backward slash, followed by special characters. These sequences represent a single character in the C language even if they are composed of more than 1 character. Examples of some of the most common escape sequences, and their integer (ASCII) value, used in C include the following:

Character	Escape Sequence	ASCII Value
Backspace	\b	008
Bell	\a	007
Newline	\n	010
Null	\o	000
Carriage	\r	013
Horizontal tab	\t	009
Vertical tab	\v	011
Form feed	\f	012

String Literals

Multibyte characters that form a sequence are called string literals. Multibyte characters have bit representations that fit into 1 or more bytes. String literals are enclosed within double quotation marks, for example, "A" and "Anna". There are 2 types of string literals, namely, UTF-8 string literals and wide string literals. Prefixes used for wide string literals include u, U or L. Prefix for UTF-8 string literals is u8.

Additional characters or extended character sets included in string literals are recognized and supported by the compiler. These additional characters can be used meaningfully to further enhance character constants and string literals.

Symbolic constants

Symbolic constants are substitute names for numeric, string or character constants within a program. The compiler would replace the symbolic constants with its actual value once the program is run.

At the beginning of the program, the symbolic constant is defined with a # **define** feature. This feature is called the preprocessor directive.

The definition of a symbolic constant does not end with a semi colon, like other C statements. Take a look at this example:

```
#define PI 3.1415
```

(//PI is the constant that will represent value 3.1415)

```
#define True 1
```

```
#define name "Alice"
```

For all numeric constants such as floating point and integer, non-numeric characters and blank spaces are not included. These constants are also limited by minimum and maximum bounds, which are usually dependent on the computer.

Variables

Memory locations where data is stored are called variables. These are indicated by a unique identifier. Names for variables are symbolic representations that refer to a particular memory location. Examples are *count, car_no* and *sum*.

Rules when writing the variable names

Writing variable names follow certain rules in order to make sure that data is stored properly and retrieved efficiently.

- Letters (in both lowercase and uppercase), underscore ('_') and digits are the only characters that can be used for variable names.

- Variables should begin either with an underscore or a letter. Starting with an underscore is acceptable, but is not highly recommended. Underscores at the beginning of variables can come in conflict with system names and the compiler may protest.

- There is no limit on the length of variables. The compiler can distinguish the first 31 characters of a variable. This means that individual variables should have different sequences for the 1st 31 characters.

Variables should also be declared at the beginning of a program before it can be used.

Chapter 2 What is C Programming Language?

In C, the programming language is a language that focuses on the structure. It was developed in 1972, at Bell Laboratories, by Dennis Ritchie. The features of the language were derived from "B", which is an earlier programming language and formally known as BCPL or Basic Combined Programming Language. The C programming language was originally developed to implement the UNIX operating system.

Standards of C Programming Language

In 1989, the American National Standards Institute developed the 1st standard specifications. This pioneering standard specification was referred to as C89 and C90, both referring to the same programming language.

In 1999, a revision was made in the programming language. The revised standard was called C99. It had new features such as advanced data types. It also had a few changes, which gave rise to more applications.

The C11 standard was developed, which added new features to the programming language for C. This had a library-like generic macro type, enhanced Unicode support, anonymous structures, multi-threading, bounds-checked functions and atomic structures. It had improved compatibility with C++. Some parts of the C99 library in C11 were made optional.

The Embedded C programming language included a few features that were not part of C. These included the named address spaces, basic I/O hardware addressing and fixed point arithmetic.

C Programming Language Features

There are a lot of features of the programming language, which include the following:

- Modularity

- Interactivity

- Portability

- Reliability

- Effectiveness

- Efficiency

- Flexibility

Uses of the C Programming Language

This language has found several applications. It is now used for the development of system applications, which form a huge portion of operating systems such as Linux, Windows and UNIX.

Some of the applications of C language include the following:

- Spreadsheets

- Database systems

- Word processors

- Graphics packages

- Network drivers

- Compilers and Assemblers

- Operating system development

- Interpreters

Chapter 3 Understanding C Program

The C program has several features and steps in order for an output or function is carried out.

Basic Commands (for writing basic C Program)

The basic syntax and commands used in writing a simple C program include the following:

#include <stdio.h>

This command is a preprocessor. <stdio.h> stands for standard input output header file. This is a file from the C library, which is included before the C program is compiled.

int main()

Execution of all C program begins with this main function.

{

This symbol is used to indicate the start of the main function.

}

This indicates the conclusion of the main function.

/* */

Anything written in between this command will not be considered for execution and compilation.

printf (output);

The printf command prints the output on the screen.

getch();

Writing this command would allow the system to wait for any keyboard character input.

return 0

Writing this command will terminate the C program or main function and return to 0.

A basic C Program would look like this:

```
#include <stdio.h>
int main()
{
/* Our first simple C basic program */
printf("Hello People! ");
getch();
return 0;
}
```

The output of this simple program would look like this:

Hello People!

Chapter 4 Learn C Programming

After learning the basic elements and what the language is all about, time to start programming in C. Here are the most important steps:

Download a compiler

A compiler is a program needed to compile the C code. It interprets the written codes and translates it into specific signals, which can be understood by the computer. Usually, compiler programs are free. There are different compilers available for several operating systems. Microsoft Visual Studio and MinGW are compilers available for Windows operating systems. XCode is among the best compilers for Mac. Among the most widely used C compiler options for Linux is gcc.

Basic Codes

Consider the following example of a simple C program in the previous chapter:

```c
#include <stdio.h>


int main()

{

    printf("Hello People!\n");

    getchar();

    return 0;

}
```

At the start of the program, #include command is placed. This is important in order to load the libraries where the needed functions are located.

The <stdio.h> refers to the file library and allows for the use of the succeeding functions getchar() and printf().

The command int main () sends a message to the compiler to run the function with the name "main" and return a certain integer once it is done running. Every C program executes a main function.

The symbol { } is used to specify that everything within it is a component of the "main" function that the compiler should run.

The function printf() tells the system to display the words or characters within the parenthesis onto the computer screen. The quotation marks make certain that the C compiler would print the words or characters as it is. The sequence \n informs the C compiler to place its cursor to the succeeding line. At the conclusion of the line, a ; (semicolon) is placed to denote that the sequence is done. Most codes in C program needs a semicolon to denote where the line ends.

The command getchar() informs the compiler to stop once it reaches the end of the function and standby for an input from the keyboard before continuing. This command is very useful because most compilers would run the C program and then immediately exits the window. The getchar() command would prevent the compiler to close the window until after a keystroke .is made.

The command return 0 denotes that the function has ended. For this particular C program, it started as an int, which indicates that the program has to return an integer once it is done running. The "0" is an indication that the compiler ran the program correctly. If another number is returned at the end of the program, it means that there was an error somewhere in the program.

Compiling the program

To compile the program, type the code into the program's code editor. Save this as a type of *.c file, then click the Run or Build button.

Commenting on the code

Any comments placed on codes are not compiled. These allow the user to give details on what happens in the function. Comments are good reminders on what the code is all about and for what. Comments also help other developers to understand what the code when they look at it.

To make a comment, add a /* at the beginning of the comment. End the written comment with a */. When commenting, comment on everything except the basic portions of the code, where explanations are no longer necessary because the meanings are already clearly understood.

Also, comments can be utilized for quick removal of code parts without having to delete them. Just enclose portions of the code in /* */, then compile. Remove these tags if these portions are to be added back into the code.

USING VARIABLES

Understanding variables

Define the variables before using them. Some common ones include char, float and int.

Declaring variables

Again, variables have to be declared before the program can use them. To declare, enter data type and then the name of the variable. Take a look at these examples:

```
char name;

float x;

int f, g, i, j;
```

Multiple variables can also be declared all on a single line, on condition that all of them belong to the same data type. Just separate the names of the variables commas (i.e., int f, g, i, j;).

When declaring variables, always end the line with a semicolon to denote that the line has ended.

Location on declaring the variables

Declaring variables is done at the start of the code block. This is the portion of the code enclosed by the brackets {}. The program won't function well if variables are declared later within the code block.

Variables for storing user input

Simple programs can be written using variables. These programs will store inputs of the user. Simple programs will use the function scanf, which searches the user's input for particular values. Take a look at this example:

```
#include <stdio.h>


int main()

{

int x;


printf( "45: " );

scanf( "%d", &x );

printf( "45 %d", x );

getchar();

return 0;

}
```

The string &d informs the function scanf to search the input for any integers.

The command & placed before the x variable informs the function scanf where it can search for the specific variable so that the function can change it. It also informs the function to store the defined integer within the variable.

The last printf tells the compiler to read back the integer input into the screen as a feedback for the user to check.

Manipulating variables

Mathematical expressions can be used, which allow users to manipulate stored variables. When using mathematical expressions, it is most important to remember to use the "=" distinction. A single = will set the variable's value. A == (double equal sign) is placed when the goal is to compare the values on both sides of the sign, to check if the values are equal.

For example:

x = 2 * 4; /* sets the value of "x" to 2 * 4, or 8 */

x = x + 8; /* adds 8 to the original "x " value, and defines the new "x" value as the specific variable */

x == 18; /* determines if the value of "x" is equal to 18 */

x < 11; /* determines if the "x" value is lower than 11 */

CONDITIONAL STATEMENTS

Conditional statements can also be used within the C program. In fact, most programs are driven by these statements. These are determined as either False or True and then acted upon depending on the results. The most widely used and basic conditional statement is if.

In C, False and True statements are treated differently. Statements that are "TRUE" are those that end up equal to nonzero numbers. For example, when a comparison is performed, the outcome is a "TRUE" statement if the returned numerical value is "1". The result is a "FALSE" statement if the value that returns is "0".

Basic conditional operators

The operation of conditional statements is based on mathematical operators used in comparing values. The most common conditional operators include the following:

< /* less than */

6 < 15 TRUE

> /* greater than */

10 > 5 TRUE

<= /* less than or equal to */

4 <= 8 TRUE

>= /* greater than or equal to */

8 >= 8 TRUE

!= /* not equal to */

4 != 5 TRUE

== /* equal to */

7 == 7 TRUE

How to write a basic "IF" conditional statement

A conditional "IF" statement is used in determining what the next step in the program is after evaluation of the statement. These can be combined with other types of conditional statements in order to create multiple and powerful options.

Take a look at this example:

```
#include <stdio.h>


int main()

{

if ( 4 < 7 )

    printf( "4 is less than 7");

    getchar();

}
```

The "ELSE/ELSE IF" statements

These statements can be used in expanding the conditional statements. Build upon the "IF" statements with "ELSE" and "ELSE IF" type of conditional statements, which will handle different types of results. An "ELSE" statement will be run when the IF statement result is FALSE. An "ELSE IF" statement will allow for the inclusion of multiple IF statements in one code block, which will handle all the various cases of the statement.

Take a look at this example:

```c
#include <stdio.h>

int main()
{
int age;

printf( "Please type current age: " );
scanf( "%d", &age );
if ( age <= 10 ) {
printf( "You are just a kid!\n" );
}
else if ( age < 30 ) {
printf( "Being a young adult is pretty awesome!\n" );
}
else if ( age < 50 ) {
printf( "You are young at heart!\n" );
}
else {
printf( "Age comes with wisdom.\n" );
}
return 0;
```

```
}
```

The above program will take all the input from the user and will run it through the different defined IF statements. If the input (number) satisfies the 1st IF statement, the 1st printf statement will be returned. If it does not, then input will be run through each of the "ELSE IF" statements until a match is found. If after all the "ELSE IF" statements have been run and nothing works, the input will be run through the "ELSE" statement at the last part of the program.

LOOPS

Loops are among the most important parts of C programming. These allow the user to repeat code blocks until particular conditions have been met. Loops make implementing repeated actions easy and reduce the need to write new conditional statements each time.

There are 3 main types of loops in C programming. These are FOR, WHILE and Do... WHILE.

"FOR" Loop

The "FOR" loop is the most useful and commonly used type of loop in C programming. This loop continues to run the function until the conditions set for this loop are met. There are 3 conditions required by the FOR loop. These include initialization of the variable, meeting the condition and how updating of the variable is done. All of these conditions need not be met at the same time, but a blank space with semicolon is still needed to prevent the loop from running continuously.

Take a look at this example:

```
#include <stdio.h>


int main()

{

int y;


for ( y = 0; y < 10; y++;){
```

```
    printf( "%d\n", y );

}

    getchar();

}
```

The value of y has been set to 0, and the loop is programmed to continue running as long as the y value remains less than 10. At each run (loop), the y value is increased by 1 before the loop is repeated. Hence, once the value of y is equivalent to 10 (after 10 loops), the above loop will then break.

WHILE Loop

These are simpler than the FOR loops. There is only one condition, which is that as long as the condition remains TRUE, the loop continues to run. Variables need not to be initialized or updated, but can be done within the loop's main body.

Take a look at this example:

```
#include <stdio.h>


int main()

{

int y;


while ( y <= 20 ){

    printf( "%d\n", y );

    y++;

}
```

```
getchar();

}
```

In the above program, the command y++ will add 1 to the variable *y* for each execution of the loop. When the value of *y* reaches 21, the loop will break.

DO...WHILE Loop

This is a very useful loop to ensure at least 1 run. FOR and WHILE loops check the conditions at the start of the loop, which ensures that it could not immediately pass and fail. DO...WHILE loops will check the conditions when the loop is finished. This ensures that the loop will run at last once before a pass and fail occurs.

Take a look at this example:

```
#include <stdio.h>


int main()

{

int y;


y = 10;

do {

printf("This loop is running!\n");

} while ( y != 10 );

getchar();

}
```

This type of loop displays the message whether the condition results turn out TRUE or FALSE. The *y* variable is set to 10. The WHILE loop has been set to run when the y value is not equal to 10, at which the loop ends. The message was printed because the condition is not checked until the loop has ended.

The WHILE portion of the DO..WHILE loop must end with a semicolon. This is also the only instance when a loop ends this way.

Conclusion

Thank you again for purchasing this book!

I hope this book was able to help you to understand the complex terms and language used in C. this programming method can put off a lot of users because of its seemingly complexity. However, with the right basic knowledge, soon, you will be programming more complex things with C.

The next step is to start executing these examples. Reading and understanding this book is not enough, although this will push you into the right direction. Execution will cement the knowledge and give you the skill and deeper understanding of C.

Finally, if you enjoyed this book, please take the time to share your thoughts and post a review on Amazon. We do our best to reach out to readers and provide the best value we can. Your positive review will help us achieve that. It'd be greatly appreciated!

Thank you and good luck!

Book 2
Android Programming In a Day!

BY SAM KEY

The Power Guide for Beginners In Android App Programming

Table Of Contents

Introduction.. 35

Chapter 1Preparation 36

Chapter 2Starting Your First Project 38

Chapter 3Getting Familiar with Eclipse and Contents of an Android App.. 43

Chapter 4Running Your Program 47

Conclusion 50

Check Out My Other Books 51

Chapter 1: Preparation

Android application development is not easy. You must have some decent background in program development. It is a plus if you know Visual Basic and Java. And it will be definitely a great advantage if you are familiar or have already used Eclipse's IDE (Integrated Development Environment). Also, being familiar with XML will help you.

You will need a couple of things before you can start developing apps.

First, you will need a high-end computer. It is common that other programming development kits do not need a powerful computer in order to create applications. However, creating programs for Android is a bit different. You will need more computing power for you to run Android emulators, which are programs that can allow you to test your programs in your computer.

Using a weak computer without a decent processor and a good amount of RAM will only make it difficult for you to run those emulators. If you were able to run it, it will run slowly.

Second, you will need an Android device. That device will be your beta tester. With it, you will know how your program will behave in an Android device. When choosing the test device, make sure that it is at par with the devices of the market you are targeting for your app. If you are targeting tablet users, use a tablet. If you are targeting smartphones, then use a smartphone.

Third, you will need the Android SDK (Software Development Kit) from Google. The SDK is a set of files and programs that can allow you to create and compile your program's code. As of this writing, the latest Android SDK's file size is around 350mb. It will take you 15 – 30 minutes to download it. If you uncompressed the Android SDK file, it will take up around 450mb of your computer's disk space. The link to the download page is: http://developer.android.com/sdk/index.html

The SDK can run on Windows XP, Windows 7, Mac OSX 10.8.5 (or higher), and Linux distros that can run 32bit applications and has glibc (GNU C library) 2.11 or higher.

Once you have unpacked the contents of the file you downloaded, open the SDK Manager. That program is the development kit's update tool. To make sure you have the latest versions of the kit's components, run the manager once in a while and download those updates. Also, you can use the SDK Manager to download older versions of SDK. You must do that in case you want to make programs with devices with dated Android operating systems.

Chapter 2: Starting Your First Project

To start creating programs, you will need to open Eclipse. The Eclipse application file can be found under the eclipse folder on the extracted files from the Android SDK. Whenever you run Eclipse, it will ask you where you want your Eclipse workspace will be stored. You can just use the default location and just toggle the don't show checkbox.

New Project

To start a new Android application project, just click on the dropdown button of the New button on Eclipse's toolbar. A context menu will appear, and click on the Android application project.

The New Android Application project details window will appear. In there, you will need to input some information for your project. You must provide your program's application name, project name, and package name. Also, you can configure the minimum and target SDK where your program can run and the SDK that will be used to compile your code. And lastly, you can indicate the default theme that your program will use.

Application Name

The application name will be the name that will be displayed on the Google's Play Store when you post it there. The project name will be more of a file name for Eclipse. It will be the project's identifier. It should be unique for every project that you build in Eclipse. By default, Eclipse will generate a project and package name for your project when you type something in the Application Name text box.

Package Name

The package name is not usually displayed for users. Take note that in case you will develop a large program, you must remember that your package name should never be changed. On the other hand, it is common that package names are the reverse of your domain name plus your project's name. For example, if your website's domain name is www.mywebsite.com and your project's name is Hello World, a good package name for your project will be com.mywebsite.helloworld.

The package name should follow the Java package name convention. The naming convention is there to prevent users from having similar names, which could result to numerous conflicts. Some of the rules you need to follow for the package name are:

•   Your package name should be all in lower caps. Though Eclipse will accept a package name with a capital letter, but it is still best to adhere to standard practice.

•   The reverse domain naming convention is included as a standard practice.

•   Avoid using special characters in the package name. Instead, you can replace it with underscores.

•   Also, you should never use or include the default com.example in your package name. Google Play will not accept an app with a package name like that.

Minimum SDK

Minimum required SDK could be set to lower or the lowest version of Android. Anything between the latest and the set minimum required version can run your program. Setting it to the lowest, which is API 1 or Android 1.0, can make your target audience wider.

Setting it to Android 2.2 (Froyo) or API 8, can make your program run on almost 95% of all Android devices in the world. The drawback fn this is that the features you can include in your program will be limited. Adding new features will force your minimum required SDK to move higher since some of the new functions in Android is not available on lower versions of the API (Application Programming Interface).

Target SDK

The target SDK should be set to the version of Android that most of your target audience uses. It indicates that you have tested your program to that version. And it means that your program is fully functional if they use it on a device that runs the target Android version.

Whenever a new version of Android appears, you should also update the target SDK of your program. Of course, before you release it to the market again, make sure that you test it on an updated device.

If a device with the same version as your set target SDK runs your program, it will not do any compatibility behavior or adjust itself to run the program. By default, you should set it to the highest version to attract your potential app buyers. Setting a lower version for your target SDK would make your program old and dated. By the way, the target SDK should be always higher or equal with the minimum target SDK version.

Compile with

The compile with version should be set to the latest version of Android. This is to make sure that your program will run on almost all versions down to the minimum version you have indicated, and to take advantage of the newest features and optimization offered by the latest version of Android. By default, the Android SDK will only have one version available for this option, which is API 20 or Android 4.4 (KitKat Wear).

After setting those all up, it is time to click on the Next button. The new page in the screen will contain some options such as creating custom launcher icon and creating activity. As of now, you do not need to worry about those. Just leave the default values and check, and click the Next button once again.

Custom Launcher Icon

Since you have left the Create Custom Launcher option checked, the next page will bring you in the launcher icon customization page. In there, you will be given three options on how you would create your launcher. Those options are launcher icons made from an image, clipart, or text.

With the text and clipart method, you can easily create an icon you want without thinking about the size and quality of the launcher icon. With those two, you can just get a preset image from the SDK or Android to use as a launcher icon. The same goes with the text method since all you need is to type the letters you want to appear on the icon and the SDK will generate an icon based on that.

The launcher icon editor also allows you to change the background and foreground color of your icon. Also, you can scale the text and clipart by changing the value of the additional padding of the icon. And finally, you can add simple 3D shapes on your icon to make it appear more professional.

Bitmap Iconography Tips

When it comes to images, you need to take note of a few reminders. First, always make sure that you will use vector images. Unlike the typical bitmap images (pictures taken from cameras or images created using Paint), vector images provide accurate and sharp images. You can scale it multiple times, but its sharpness will not disappear and will not pixelate. After all, vector images do not contain information about pixels. It only has numbers and location of the colors and lines that will appear in it. When it is scaled, it does not perform antialiasing or stretching since its image will be mathematically rendered.

In case that you will be the one creating or designing the image that you will use for your program and you will be creating a bitmap image, make sure that you start with a large image. A large image is easier to create and design.

Also, since in Android, multiple sizes of your icon will be needed, a large icon can make it easier for you to make smaller ones. Take note that if you scale a big picture into a small one, some details will be lost, but it will be easier to edit and fix and it will still look crisp. On the other hand, if you scale a small image into a big one, it will pixelate and insert details that you do not intend to show such as jagged and blurred edges.

Nevertheless, even when scaling down a big image into a smaller one, do not forget to rework the image. Remember that a poor-looking icon makes people think that the app you are selling is low-quality. And again, if you do not want to go through all that, create a vector image instead.

Also, when you create an image, make sure that it will be visible in any background. Aside from that, it is advisable to make it appear uniform with other Android icons. To do that, make sure that your image has a distinct silhouette that will make it look like a 3D image. The icon should appear as if you were looking above it and as if the source of light is on top of the image. The topmost part of the icon should appear lighter and the bottom part should appear darker.

Activity

Once you are done with your icon, click on the Next button. The page will now show the Activity window. It will provide you with activity templates to work on. The window has a preview box where you can see what your app will look like for every activity template. Below the selection, there is a description box that will tell you what each template does. For now, select the Blank Activity and click Next. The next page will ask you some details regarding the activity. Leave it on its default values and click Finish.

Once you do that, Eclipse will setup your new project. It might take a lot of time, especially if you are using a dated computer. The next chapter will discuss the programming interface of Eclipse.

Chapter 3: Getting Familiar with Eclipse and Contents of an Android App

When Eclipse has finished its preparation, you will be able to start doing something to your program. But hold onto your horses; explore Eclipse first before you start fiddling with anything.

Editing Area

In the middle of the screen, you will see a preview of your program. In it, you will see your program's icon beside the title of your program. Just left of it is the palette window. It contains all the elements that you can place in your program.

Both of these windows are inside Eclipse's editing area. You will be spending most of your time here, especially if you are going to edit or view something in your code or layout.

The form widgets tab will be expanded in the palette by default. There you will see the regular things you see in an Android app such as buttons, radio buttons, progress bar (the circle icon that spins when something is loading in your device or the bar the fills up when your device is loading), seek bar, and the ratings bar (the stars you see in reviews).

Aside from the form widgets, there are other elements that you can check and use. Press the horizontal tabs or buttons and examine all the elements you can possibly use in your program.

To insert a widget in your program, you can just drag the element you want to include from the palette and drop it in your program's preview. Eclipse will provide you visual markers and grid snaps for you to place the widgets you want on the exact place you want. Easy, right?

Take note, some of the widgets on the palette may require higher-level APIs or versions of Android. For example, the Grid Layout from the Layouts section of the palette requires API 14 (Android 4.0 Ice Cream Sandwich) or higher. If you add it in your program, it will ask you if you want to install it. In case you did include and install it, remember that it will not be compatible for older versions or any device running on API 13 and lower. It is advisable that you do not include any element that asks for installation. It might result into errors.

Output Area, Status Bar, and Problem Browser

On the bottom part of Eclipse, the status bar, problem browser, and output area can be found. It will contain messages regarding to the state of your project. If Eclipse found errors in your program, it will be listed there. Always check the Problems bar for any issues. Take note that you cannot run or compile your program if Eclipse finds at least one error on your project.

Navigation Pane

On the leftmost part of your screen is the navigation pane that contains the package explorer. The package explorer lets you browse all the files that are included in your project. Three of the most important files that you should know where to look for are:

•   activity_main.xml: This file is your program's main page or window. And it will be the initial file that will be opened when you create a new project. In case you accidentally close it on your editor window, you can find it at: YourProjectName > res > layout > activity_main.xml.

•   MainActivity.java: As of now, you will not need to touch this file. However, it is important to know where it is since later in your Android development activities, you will need to understand it and its contents. It is located at: YourProjectName > src > YourPackageName > MainActivity.java.

44

• AndroidManifest.xml: It contains the essential information that you have set up a while ago when you were creating your project file in Eclipse. You can edit the minimum and target SDK in there. It is located at YourProjectName > AndroidManifest.xml.

Aside from those files, you should take note of the following directories:

• src/: This is where most of your program's source files will be placed. And your main activity file is locafile is located.

• res/: Most of the resources will be placed here. The resources are placed inside the subdirectories under this folder.

• res/drawable-hdpi/: Your high density bitmap files that you might show in your app will go in here.

• res/layout/: All the pages or interface in your app will be located here – including your activity_main.xml.

• res/values/: The values you will store and use in your program will be placed in this directory in form of XML files.

In the event that you will create multiple projects, remember that the directory for those other projects aside from the one you have opened will still be available in your package explorer. Because of that, you might get confused over the files you are working on. Thankfully, Eclipse's title bar indicates the location and name of the file you are editing, which makes it easier to know what is currently active on the editing area.

Outline Box

Displays the current structure of the file you are editing. The outline panel will help you visualize the flow and design of your app. Also, it can help you find the widgets you want to edit.

Properties Box

Whenever you are editing a layout file, the properties box will appear below the outline box. With the properties box, you can edit certain characteristics of a widget. For example, if you click on the Hello World text on the preview of your main activity layout file, the contents of the properties box will be populated. In there, you can edit the properties of the text element that you have clicked. You can change the text, height, width, and even its font color.

Menu and Toolbar

The menu bar contains all the major functionalities of Eclipse. In case you do not know where the button of a certain tool is located, you can just invoke that tool's function on the menu bar. On the other hand, the tool bar houses all the major functions in Eclipse. The most notable buttons there are the New, Save, and Run.

As of now, look around Eclipse's interface. Also, do not do or change anything on the main activity file or any other file. The next chapter will discuss about how to run your program. As of now, the initial contents of your project are also valid as an android program. Do not change anything since you might produce an unexpected error. Nevertheless, if you really do want to change something, go ahead. You can just create another project for you to keep up with the next chapter.

Chapter 4: Running Your Program

By this time, even if you have not done anything yet to your program, you can already run and test it in your Android device or emulator. Why teach this first before the actual programming? Well, unlike typical computer program development, Android app development is a bit bothersome when it comes to testing.

First, the program that you are developing is intended for Android devices. You cannot actually run it normally in your computer without the help of an emulator. And you will actually do a lot of testing. Even with the first lines of code or changes in your program, you will surely want to test it.

Second, the Android emulator works slow. Even with good computers, the emulator that comes with the Android SDK is painstakingly sluggish. Alternatively, you can use BlueStacks. BlueStacks is a free Android emulator that works better than the SDK's emulator. It can even run games with it! However, it is buggy and does not work well (and does not even run sometimes) with every computer.

This chapter will focus on running your program into your Android device. You will need to have a USB data cable and connect your computer and Android. Also, you will need to have the right drivers for your device to work as a testing platform for the programs you will develop. Unfortunately, this is the preferred method for most beginners since running your app on Android emulators can bring a lot more trouble since it is super slow. And that might even discourage you to continue Android app development.

Why Android Emulators are Slow

Why are Android emulators slow? Computers can run virtual OSs without any problems, but why cannot the Android emulator work fine? Running virtual OSs is not something as resource-extensive anymore with today's computer standards. However, with Android, you will actually emulate an OS together with a mobile device. And nowadays, these mobile devices are as powerful as some of the dated computers back then. Regular computers will definitely have a hard time with that kind of payload from an Android emulator.

USB Debugging Mode

To run your program in an Android device, connect your Android to your computer. After that, set your Android into USB debugging mode. Depending on the version of the Android device you are using, the steps might change.

For 3.2 and older Android devices:

Go to Settings > Applications > Development

For 4.0 and newer Android devices:

Go to Settings > Developer Options

For 4.2 and newer Android devices with hidden Developer Options:

Go to Settings > About Phone. After that, tap the Build Number seven times. Go back to the previous screen. The Developer Options should be visible now.

Android Device Drivers

When USB debugging is enabled, your computer will install the right drivers for the Android device that you have. If your computer does not have the right drivers, you will not be able to run your program on your device. If that happens to you, visit this page: http://developer.android.com/tools/extras/oem-usb.html. It contains instructions on how you can install the right driver for your device and operating system.

Running an App in Your Android Device Using Eclipse

Once your device is already connected and you have the right drivers for it, you can now do a test run of your application. On your Eclipse window, click the Run button on the toolbar or in the menu bar.

If a Run As window appeared, select the Android Application option and click on the OK button. After that, a dialog box will appear. It will provide you with two options: running the program on an Android device or on an AVD (Android Virtual Device) or emulator.

If your device was properly identified by your computer, it will appear on the list. Click on your device's name and click OK. Eclipse will compile your Android app, install it on your device, and then run it. That is how simple it is.

Take note, there will be times that your device will appear offline on the list. In case that happens, there are two simple fixes that you can do to make it appear online again: restart your device or disable and enable the USB debugging function on your device.

Now, you can start placing widgets on your main activity file. However, always make sure that you do not place any widgets that require higher APIs.

Conclusion

Thank you again for purchasing this book!

I hope this book was able to help you get started with Android Programming in a Day!.

The next step is to study the following:

View and Viewgroups: View and Viewgroups are the two types of objects that you will be dealing with Android. View objects are the elements or widgets that you see in Android programs. Viewgroup objects act as containers to those View objects.

Relative, Linear, and Table Layout: When it comes to designing your app, you need to know the different types of layouts. In later versions of Android, you can use other versions of layouts, but of course, the API requirements will go up if you use them. Master these, and you will be able to design faster and cleaner.

Adding Activities or Interface: Of course, you would not want your program to contain one page only. You need more. You must let your app customers to see more content and functions. In order to do that, you will need to learn adding activities to your program. This is the part when developing your Android app will be tricky. You will not be able to rely completely on the drag and drop function and graphical layout view of Eclipse. You will need to start typing some code into your program.

Adding the Action Bar: The action bar is one of the most useful elements in Android apps. It provides the best location for the most used functions in your program. And it also aid your users when switching views, tabs, or drop down list.

Once you have gain knowledge on those things, you will be able to launch a decent app on the market. The last thing you might want to do is to learn how to make your program support other Android devices.

You must know very well that Android devices come in all shapes and form. An Android device can be a tablet, a smartphone, or even a television. Also, they come with different screen sizes. You cannot just expect that all your customers will be using a 4-inch display smartphone. Also, you should think about the versions of Android they are using. Lastly, you must also add language options to your programs. Even though English is fine, some users will appreciate if your program caters to the primary language that they use.

Introduction

I want to thank you and congratulate you for purchasing the book, "Introduction to Android Programming in a Day – The Power Guide for Beginners in Android App Programming".

This book contains proven steps and strategies on how to get started with Android app development.

This book will focus on preparing you with the fun and tiring world of Android app development. Take note that this book will not teach you on how to program. It will revolve around the familiarization of the Android SDK and Eclipse IDE.

Why not focus on programming immediately? Unfortunately, the biggest reason many aspiring Android developers stop on learning this craft is due to the lack of wisdom on the Android SDK and Eclipse IDE.

Sure, you can also make apps using other languages like Python and other IDEs on the market. However, you can expect that it is much more difficult than learning Android's SDK and Eclipse's IDE.

On the other hand, you can use tools online to develop your Android app for you. But where's the fun in that? You will not learn if you use such tools. Although it does not mean that you should completely stay away from that option.

Anyway, the book will be split into four chapters. The first will prepare you and tell you the things you need before you develop apps. The second will tell you how you can configure your project. The third will introduce you to the Eclipse IDE. And the last chapter will teach you on how to run your program in your Android device.

Also, this book will be sprinkled with tidbits about the basic concepts of Android app development. And as you read along, you will have an idea on what to do next.

Thanks again for purchasing this book, I hope you enjoy it!

And that is about it for this book. Make sure you do not stop learning Android app development.

Finally, if you enjoyed this book, please take the time to share your thoughts and post a review on Amazon. We do our best to reach out to readers and provide the best value we can. Your positive review will help us achieve that. It'd be greatly appreciated!

Thank you and good luck!

Check Out My Other Books

Below you'll find some of my other popular books that are popular on Amazon
and Kindle as well. Simply click on the links below to check them out.
Alternatively, you can visit my author page on Amazon to see other work done by
me.

the rest of C Programming Success in a Day

If the links do not work, for whatever reason, you can simply search for these
titles on the Amazon website to find them.

www.ingramcontent.com/pod-product-compliance
Lightning Source LLC
Chambersburg PA
CBHW061042050326
40689CB00012B/2934